SURVIVING SUICIDE BEREAVEMENT

Finding life after death

GW00778053

BRENDAN MCMANUS SJ

First published in 2016 by Messenger Publications

ISBN 978-1-910248-34-8

Designed by Messenger Publications Design Department
Typeset in Calibri
Printed by Naas Printing Ltd

MESSENGER
PUBLICATIONS
JESUITS in IRELAND

Messenger Publications,
37 Lower Leeson Street, Dublin 2
www.messenger.ie

Brendan McManus SJ lost his brother Donal to suicide in 2005 and has written and spoken extensively about his grief journey. He published an article, 'Surviving Suicide' in *The Furrow* journal, and a book, *Redemption Road*, about walking the Camino in honour of his deceased brother. Here, some ten years later, he offers advice on the complex suicide grief process and what he has found to be helpful for survival, adaptation and thriving.

The moment your world changes

It starts with the news that you never want to get, when your blood freezes and your life is changed irrevocably. It is never to return.

You are bereaved by the suicide of a loved one; it is devastating.

All your support structures are kicked away and you fall out of normal life. Your immediate task is now survival, struggling to keep afloat. It is a grief journey like no other as it touches the deepest depths of you as a person, especially your fears and crippling despair. It demands everything from your personal resources of coping, emotional well-being and resilience. However unlikely it seems at first, this furnace of suffering promises to make of you a new person. It is an enforced one-way trip, however, and it allows for no hankering back, wishing for the past or even staying the same – everything changes forever.

Initially there is the shock of what has happened and trying to function within the bizarre dream-world that is the funeral, the mourners, the expressions of support. You watch in a daze as the casket is closed and they are commended to the earth or the flames. Then there is the emptiness, the absence of the person and the pressing horror of the situation. Shock is a helpful companion to isolate yourself from the pain. Days are long and you get through, keep going and try not to think.

After a while the questions become more insistent, *'Why did they do it?'*, *'Was I not enough?'*, *'What did I do or say in those last days?'* Like a forensic detective you search for clues, endlessly pouring over those last days, reaching apparently negative conclusions. There is the regret of missed opportunities, feeling responsible, and terrible guilt fuelled by the piercing pain of loss.

Anniversaries are difficult, reminders of the person are everywhere and you surround yourself with shrines and symbols to them. They are comforting initially, but their warmth and reassurance gradually fades. You feel like screaming at God, *How was this allowed to happen? If you are so powerful and the person was so good, why did it end up bad? Where are they now and why can I not feel their presence? Please don't let them have fallen into the outer darkness of nothingness.* I have to believe that there is some hope for them, help my own fragile faith survive this spiritual pain I feel. Life becomes difficult as hell. I walk in the wasteland that was once my life.

Unable to deal with it all on your own, you ask for help for yourself. You begin to try to rebuild your life, reaching out as you wish your loved one had. Maybe you explore different therapies and support groups. Even reading this booklet is a positive step towards finding out what has helped other people cope. Very few people understand what it is like to go through the crushing mill of suicide, and it can be a relief to find even a few like-minded people who understand your journey. This booklet is a combination of the personal experience of the writer and many other resources and people referenced here.

Eventually, slowly and over a long time, there comes a day when the pain is less. A new springtime arrives in my life and I feel hope again. The person I have lost is not gone from me; rather they are with me in a new, consoling way that helps me live my new life. I feel their presence in a helpful way, not the pain of grief now, but in a deep sense of peace and direction for my life. I have come through the storm of loss, I have been tossed about by the waves and winds, and now I am in a new phase of my life where there is real calm. It has made of me a better person, compassionate and understanding, I can be really present to others and my pain is transformed into insight.

A Special Scar

Suicide grief is 'complicated' because of the level of violence normally associated with a suicide and all the thorny issues that surround taking one's own life. There is no chance to say goodbye, no closure, but rather the question 'why' is left wide open and those left behind often end up taking a lot of responsibility and feeling guilt for what happened. The grieving survivors are those who have to assume this terrible cross of suffering and extended grief. There are so many complications to this grief that many don't cope well, but rather get trapped in the cycle of negative feelings, guilt and negative thinking. The seemingly impossible goal is to move from being a victim to being a survivor.

Suicide will always be part of you and your story, and there is a way through this maze of feelings, dead ends and setbacks. Alison Wertheimer uses the poignant image of 'A Special Scar' for suicide grief: the wound will always be visible and may not be pretty, but it is only through owning it and working through this experience that healing comes. This is a serious journey of survival against the enemies of hopelessness and despair; it is not for the faint-hearted, and many others unfortunately will not understand your journey. Normally you don't have a choice, however, and have to take this 'hard road' to healing. It is important to know that it is a God of compassion (meaning 'to suffer with you') who walks with you, especially through this 'dark night of the soul'. God *appears* absent during this awful trial, which is a profound experience of the Cross and resurrection. Eventually, through surviving this great trial, there is light at the end of the tunnel, and there are great insights and wisdom to be had about the meaning of life.

Complicated Grief
Suicide grief is different to a normal loss. What makes it different is the trauma of the loss, as often there is a level of violence involved in the death. Then there are all the unanswered questions and the 'minefields' that lengthen the process. Grief was very unpredictable for me: I thought I had moved on, but would slide deeper into a mysterious darkness. Grief is often thought of as a process, a series of steps or experiences with different characteristics and different challenges over time. However, after suicide there is no set time, structure or correct way to do it; you have to trust yourself to find your own way. This grief process affects us deeply as human beings, at all levels of our being: physical, emotional, social and spiritual. The body struggles to come to terms with this traumatic reality, and only over time does it allow healing to take place, so it is important to be gentle with ourselves and let it develop as it should. This means you can expect to feel drained, out of sorts, to have mood swings and tears, to accept feeling empty, without wishing it were different. Some basic awareness meditation mentioned later may be useful here.

We can run into problems if we try to shortcut the process or don't respect it, or try to cling to the security of earlier stages that we may have outgrown. Of special note is that the stages are not linear (i.e. that one comes in a fixed sequence after the other, e.g. shock, denial, anger, depression[2]). Given suicide bereavement's complexity and erratic nature, there is no scale to measure progress against. It is often more like a spiral whereby feelings fluctuate and change, you move backwards and forwards erratically, but there is movement in the long term. Staying balanced in the middle of these shifting sands is challenging to say the least, making sure that you don't identify too much with your feelings.[3] The challenge for the suicide bereaved is to keep positive and hopeful even when things seem not to have moved on.

Herein lies the complicated nature of suicide grief. It is a particularly challenging process. Keeping hope alive is the challenge as suicide grief imposes a huge load on survivors, with only very brief glimpses of release. It really tests us, purifies our motivations and personalities, and makes of us very different people. There is a way through but it demands everything, all our resources and creativity. Think of it as being reshaped in the depths of your humanity, painful but purifying. I describe it like 'being purified in the crucible of pain', or like gold that is tested in fire[4] that, once gone through, no longer seems threatening. Surviving suicide means you can survive anything.

The funeral
A suicide will impact different people in the family differently, depending on their relationship with the person. Within families the temptation is to not discuss the death, and people can become isolated as the distance grows between people. Add to that the emotional confusion that many have about their ambivalent feelings sur-

rounding the suicide, and you have a cocktail of emotions that is very difficult to manage. However, communication is key to healthy adaptation and it can draw families closer together. It is important to respect that different people grieve in different ways and at different times.

It is a good thing to see the body after the suicide, in the morgue or at the wake. Though it is harrowing, it helps to accept the death and is an opportunity that needs to be gently encouraged. There is something important about touching and feeling the body of your loved one. However heart breaking, it does help with accepting the death.

It is common for close friends or family to experience feelings of acute distress before the suicide happens, a kind of a premonition. It can be very reassuring to talk about this and realise that this is normal. Also, the suicidal person almost always gives clear clues before the event; growing more distant is part of that (it certainly seems to fit in terms of my brother's withdrawal). Depression is significant: research shows two thirds of suicides had a depressive illness; 90% some kind of mental disorder. It is important not to beat oneself up about these (I missed these too), but to talk about them openly and not carry them as a 'burning secret'.

Directly after the death there is a very intense period of talking about the person, their behaviour and motivations. Though short lived it is an opportunity to witness to the life of the person, their uniqueness and talents, which are important to remember. Family members can react quite differently and great care needs to be taken to respect people's individual limits and capacity for talking about what has happened. Having a confidential sharing or faith sharing among family members can be useful here if the members are able for it. This helps deal with the sense of powerlessness for those left behind and does build a sense of solidarity. However, grief is so individual and emotions are so heightened after a death that it also can be a real mine field. For example, relatives or friends can make their presence felt at the funeral in seemingly unhelpful ways (e.g. using platitudes, such as 'I know how you feel'). That calls for a lot of patience and understanding (remember that many are out of their minds with grief too).

Feeling guilty
Even though the person who took their own life is essentially the one responsible, we, the left behind, feel implicated in some way. There is a sting in the tail with suicide that the bereaved are left carrying all the grief of loss, plus the added guilt of feeling they should have saved the person. It is very common for the survivors to feel obsessively guilty and responsible. Typically, the bereaved will rehearse the last weeks and hours before the suicide, examining their own perceived failures to act. Often they will examine their last interactions and conversations with the person, looking for clues in their words or actions.

I also had the classically corrosive guilt feelings about what had happened to my brother: Did I do enough for him? Was there some opportunity I missed? What did I say to him in that last conversation? Pouring over those last days and weeks became an obsession, a self-inflicted torture through feeling responsible for what had happened. Paradoxically, another kind of guilt was in feeling the relief after the death of not having to worry about him any more. Not having to hear about the self-destructive behaviour he was engaged in, no longer tuning into the traffic reports for fear that he had died on the roads over the weekend.

What helped me over time was the 'handing it over to God' (see below), realising that I had done as much as I could, had helped keep him going for many years, and that he was with God now – I didn't have to worry.

A Faith Crisis

Another key aspect is that of faith or spirituality; suicide of a loved one shakes you to the core and has you question everything; it is a sort of spiritual earthquake. As a priest, it brought about a huge faith crisis within me. How could I believe in a loving God faced with the horror of suicide – *how could God let this happen?* I definitely lost faith over this and went through a real dark night of the soul in my relationship with God. I was troubled by the 'why me?' question, wondering if I had done something to deserve it or was it just the randomness of 'why do bad things happen to good people'. It was only after walking the feet off myself on a remote mountain retreat, that I eventually came to understand that I had many false ideas about God and suffering[5].

I began to understand my grief as a purification of faulty images of God. These were: God being responsible for everything; God protecting me from 'bad things'[6] (faith as 'divine insurance'); and God making good things happen as long as I keep the 'rules'. Painfully over time I realised that a lot of my ideas about God and life were unhelpful. This was very challenging for me as a priest who is supposed to have these things worked out (large doses of humility and humour needed)!

Gradually, I came to understand a very different image of God that through grief; a God who is close to me, present but does not control; who is compassionate and understands suffering, and yet leaves me radically free. This is a paradox: a God of love who sits with us until we are ready to ask for help. This God understands our terrible loss, holds our deceased loved one close, and wants to free us from guilt and remorse. Mercy is the defining feature of God, not judgment. Probably the biggest lesson was that God is not in the ideal but in the real; in life and the messiness of the 'now'. The Jesuit slogan 'finding God in all things' was to take on a new meaning for me in this suicide of my brother, the most harrowing of experiences.

An experience of the Cross

It seems too easy to say that suicide bereavement is an experience of the Cross, the Passion of Christ, where Jesus suffers terribly out of love for others. It can seem like escape to another 'holy' realm to avoid the pain. But think about Jesus being with you, entering into your pain. These elements of uninvited suffering, the sheer demands of the grief process and how you are crucified in grief, means that Christ is present. Far from being remote and distant, God is intimately with us in our human experience of suffering for love of the deceased. In the Cross, we take on this unasked for suffering, understanding that Christ suffers with us in that experience, and helps us find meaning in this most punishing darkness. Initially, it is common that we should react against the imposition of this unasked for burden, questioning 'Why me, God?' and asking for this to be removed ('Take this cup away from me'[7]).

Survivors of suicide grief, more than many, will understand the experience of feeling totally abandoned by God ('My God, My God, why have you forsaken me?'[8]) and feeling alone in the blackness of despair. Crucial to the experience of the Cross, however, is understanding that God is with us in this darkest of hours, as the Father was with Christ in the garden, though hidden. In fact Jesus is to accomplish his most important mission, being faithful to love while feeling alone and deserted. Being able to pray through spiritual destitution and pain, like Jesus did, has been the lifeline for me. Praying directly with the problem, the felt absence of God helps to resolve it.

This type of prayer demands the totally different approach of abandoning yourself into the hands of God; of admitting that the situation is beyond your control and asking God to take over. Doing this means placing yourself in the hands of God, explicitly admitting that a solution is beyond yourself. Instead of 'saying prayers', your struggle with darkness and despair becomes a crucial conversation with God: 'Father, into your hands I commend my spirit' Lk 23:46. I turn my negativity and doubt into a prayer in itself. It is consoling to remember that Jesus himself has experienced this in his humanity, and suffers with us in ours. Prayer is often not a joyful and consoling experience, but rather a struggling with God and wrestling with our demons. However, it is good and authentic prayer all the same. Also, God is very near to us even though his presence is not felt. Crucially, Jesus understands the depth of our inner pain in his humanity, holds our loved one close and is with us personally in the experience. Using the Psalms, which are stories of suffering and lament, can be very helpful[9], and especially using those words that Jesus himself used in his Passion.

Pray as you are

A difficult aspect for believers is suddenly finding that you cannot pray, at least not the way you used to. Often the grief experience is so overwhelming and debilitating that you find it almost impossible to pray. The mind can fill with images and memories, emotions are turbulent, and God seems horribly absent. It is hard to work out what has happened and how to proceed in prayer. The temptation is to give up prayer, cursing God for abandoning you at the worst possible moment.

The important thing to remember is that Christ loves you exactly as you are, even if you feel like a mess. The saying '*Pray as you are and not as how you want to be*' is helpful. Just give it all to God. Allow yourself to experience guilt, hopelessness and despair; acknowledging them is enough. Denying these intense emotions makes them more difficult to deal with. If you are angry with God, let God have it – God can handle it. God is with us in everything even if we don't feel close to God. Especially during this punishing time of bereavement, it is important to see God looking at you with great compassion. Think of Jesus in the Gospel and that special way he had of looking at people[10]. It is a loving gaze that melts the hardest of hearts and reaches the deepest pain. The biggest challenge is letting go of the past and accepting a new prayer reality.

I have an emergency or survival way of praying that I use for really difficult situations when the emotions are all over the place and it feels like your head is exploding. It is often called 'mindfulness', but is also known as 'awareness' meditation[11]:

1. Be aware of the air passing through your nostrils. Feel

the touch of the air, the quality of that sensation, for example, the warmth or coldness of the air that is inhaled or exhaled.

2. Concentrate on the areas of the nostrils where this slight contact is felt. Maybe a larger quantity of air passes through one nostril rather than the other.

3. The main challenge is dealing with distractions and stray thoughts: be aware of distracting thoughts or images as soon as they arise. Use your ability to separate yourself from your thinking ('I am thinking'). See yourself as an outsider would, noticing the distractions coming and going. It's like watching clouds pass by from a window and resisting being drawn in to follow them. Just let them pass. This takes a lot of practice, to be aware and not distracted. It does help recover calm and the ability to cope.

The edge of insanity

The suicide of someone you love is like a blow to the soul that – unlike a normal wound – is invisible, goes deep inside, and takes a long time to heal. In this grief process, people often feel not normal, 'totally different', like they are going mad, and even like they are part of a 'sect' that no one else can understand. The experience is unique in that it is not like a normal bereavement, as the very traumatic element means it lasts for much longer. The healing is not an external, superficial process that is neat and tidy, but rather suicide grief asks terrible questions from survivors and demands a whole reorientation of life, love, faith, priorities and goals. You find yourself in the middle of a major overhaul you never asked for.

Like the phoenix, it is an experience of being re-created

from the ashes. There is the pain of destruction of the old, and a new being is created out of blood and tears. This grief process brings one to very dark places of disorganisation and despair, necessary for one's healing, but challenging and exhausting. It is like being on the Camino in Spain where I kept climbing one mountain after another – enjoyable in the beginning, but quickly turns to being wearing and then torturous. I felt that I was stripped bare, brought to my knees, and only then could the healing begin. There is a special blessing in store for staying the course, not being a hero and accepting help. Often there is no roadmap and one finds one's way by getting lost and praying through the darkness. There is a lot of dying to oneself. It is not a fixed, structured process, but very individual and everyone needs to find their supports, their own pace, and their own way through it.

Getting Support
Due to the complex nature of this grief, the support of family and friends is critical in the recovery process. You cannot do this on your own and it is crucial to allow others to help you. Typically, like me, you will struggle with asking for help for whatever reasons of privacy, pride or personality. In difficult situations however, you have to know when your own efforts are insufficient and when to seek help. There is a great wisdom in knowing when to seek advice and support – it is a strength, not a weakness. Stigma or concern about what others think can weigh heavily. What I found helpful for me personally was realising that my brother had never really sought help until it was too late (i.e. crisis admittance in emergency departments) and I resolved that I would ask for every kind of help that

I could get. I would do the opposite of what my brother did, I was determined that *I* would learn the lesson. I would take any counselling, support or advice that would help. There is a certain amount of humility involved in doing so that does not come easily, but it does help in the long term.

The first port of call is often having close friends who listen – people who understand compassion and have been through difficulties themselves. Sometimes a grieving person just needs to be with another; even though nothing is said, all is understood. Acceptance and silent acknowledgement can go a long way and words are not always necessary. At other times an embrace is enough to indicate support, 'touch can be as healing as words'. However, care is needed in terms of who you share with as a lot of other people find it difficult to cope with suicide, as it activates people's nightmares, fears and feelings of panic. Forgiving those who find it too much or react badly is a useful skill to develop, remembering that it is not you personally they are rejecting.

There is often a need for professional suicide/grief related help, this involves referral through a GP or making contact with an approved service. Normally this takes time and trust has to be built up with a counsellor. Typically there is a certain amount of work or 'processing' that has to be done, and there are no easy solutions, miracle cures, or pat formulas that will work. There are a lot of services available these days and the hard thing can be finding one that is professional and fits your needs – you may have to work through several before you get one that works. The advantage of professional grief work is that it helps work through the conflicting feelings of love and anger towards the person, issues impossible to do on your own. Treat it as a job you have to do, don't get too complacent or too anxious about it, it will help in the long run.

Surviving the autopsy report
Another difficult moment was the arrival of the coroner's report. This was basically a medical report of the autopsy, but nothing could have prepared me for the shock of seeing that first page with my brother's name on the top and then a huge box of white space in the middle with the words 'CAUSE OF DEATH: HANGING'. It sent me into a spin that took me several days to get over.

The brutality of the clinical language and the reduction of a human being to the mechanics of death, and the various tests and examinations carried out were insensitive in the extreme. I was angry after I got over the shock of seeing it. After all, this was my brother they were talking about, in clinical, detached terms. It was as if he were an anonymous body, casually examined and written off as just another suicide case. I was angry at the medical profession's lack of compassion and basic humanity, for inflicting such suffering on family members with such a blasé attitude and reductionist approach to a human being. I still can hardly bring myself to look at that report – 'is this all that my brother amounts to?' was my question – what about the humour, the intelligence, the generosity, the whole personality that they never knew?

In some cases there is an inquest to be attended, which can be equally traumatic and needs to be thought out in advance.

Seek out fellow sufferers

Out of desperation and the need to talk to someone who understood, I went to a Console support group in Dublin (in fact, I went to an AWARE group first and when I mentioned suicide I was directed to Console; this was difficult to take at the time, but I was not going to be put off[12].) The fact that Console was a suicide support group meant that it was a safe place to be myself, express my feelings, and share with peers who had lived through the same horror. Just knowing someone was listening, who would listen without judgement, was a lifesaver. It meant that I could talk freely about my personal loss, not in my role as a priest specifically, but as another member of the group. I came away from those meetings reeling from the weight of people's tragedies, but strangely renewed to have witnessed such honesty. Most encouraging was realising there was hope, a deep healing process that eventually weighed in. Over time I could see people shift and move, often not fully healed but managing to get by. It's often just about having a place to get out the toxic feelings with those who have been there. Understandably, people sometimes find it difficult to accept help from those who haven't experienced suicide themselves; a suicide bereaved support group[13] can help with providing a safe space, mutual support and role models for how to survive the process.

The 'Why' question

The most difficult thing about suicide is trying to understand 'why'. The nature of the death leads to asking, 'what was (s)he going through', 'what pressures were they under' and 'what exactly pushed them to take their life'. This can sound strange to others not directly involved, but trying to understand what 'caused' the suicide is a tormenting obsession. The logic goes: 'if I only knew what caused him/her to go over the edge, then I would be able to rest at peace.' The problem is that it is almost impossible to know what goes through a person's head in situations of extreme stress and anguish. It is an awful temptation to think that I can go around gathering clues, talking to people, dwelling on last words or written notes, and somehow piece together a plausible explanation. Finally, the idea that this will bring some sort of closure or resolution is an illusion – there is no logical answer or neat solution to the absurdity of suicide.

I spent a lot of time trying to find out 'Why?' quizzing my brother's friends, and especially trying to locate one friend who had been closest to him. I managed to track down a family relative who appeared to offer the information I wanted. It was a dark, bleak, unfulfilling experience however. During this process, I had a strong sense of the futility of my obsession – that I was going further into a dark hole and that God was not in this endless search[14]. This helped me understand that I was trapped in an impossible desperate search (i.e. not from God) and that there was nothing I would learn that would really help me. I was able to let go of this whole pointless searching and eventually come to some peace.

Searching for clues can become an obsession, questioning people and even reading books on suicide, but eventually one has to 'let go and let God'. This is a letting go of the illusion of control, accepting that only in God is the answer found, and God's forgiveness and resolution is enough. It is a relief to give up this pointless search.

Are they in Hell?

'Is my brother in Hell?' are the most chilling words from a family member that stay with me from the funeral. Worry about negative religious consequences and eternal punishment for the person is par for the course and needs to be addressed. Some theological assistance and pastoral guidance is helpful here, in many cases old theological attitudes and negative 'divine' judgments revolve around suicide survivors.[15] Unfortunately it is still the case that feelings of shame and social stigma can prevent many people from getting the support they need, particularly getting free of guilt.

It is true that without the insights of modern psychology, suicide was seen in a harsh way (eternal damnation). However, the New Catechism of the Catholic Church has a helpful statement: '*Grave psychological disturbances, anguish, or grave fear of hardship, suffering, or torture can diminish the responsibility of the one committing suicide. We should not despair of the eternal salvation of persons who have taken their own lives.*[16]' The role of depression[17], so obvious in the case of my brother, was clearly a major contributor for this self-destructive act that largely reduced his responsibility and therefore the implication of serious mortal sin. I believe that anyone who takes their life is not in their right mind and normally is acting under extreme mental anguish.

Technically, for a sin to be mortal (meriting damnation) the act of taking one's own life has to meet three conditions[18]: it must be a grave or serious issue; the person must know that this is wrong; and the person must intentionally consent to this action. In many cases of suicide, the person is not in their right mind to give full consent.

Recent studies highlight the social and personal circumstances in suicides and show that they are rarely voluntary acts and so, while they may be mistaken and morally wrong, they are not always blameworthy. Fear, pressure, ignorance, addiction, and psychological problems can impede the exercise of the will so that a person may not be fully responsible for an action. While suicide can be judged immoral, the degree of responsibility for suicide depends upon the state of the person's mind.

Think of a fire emergency in a tower block where desperate people are forced to jump out windows to escape the inferno. They don't want to die, but have no choice as they are in an intolerably extreme situation. Similarly in suicide, the person's mind is in such a state of chaos and frenzy that they want to escape it at all costs, even if it means destroying themselves. The internal agony caused by the 'fire' of negativity, ruminations and self-hate can never be underestimated.

The Irish Catholic Bishops adopt a similar line: '*While we believe that God is the giver of life, and he alone has the right to decide when that life should end we also realise that God can look deep within the human heart, recognise its difficulties, understand and forgive.*'[19] Helpful as these sources are, it is still common to find old theological ideas and harsh condemnation of suicide victims are ingrained and prevalent. Indeed, in the funeral and afterwards, it takes courage to talk openly about suicide[20] while refusing to accept the stigma of it.

While Pope Francis hasn't written directly on suicide, it is safe to assume that his attitude would be one of compassion and concern for those left with burdens, portraying a God of mercy and forgiveness who embraces the deceased, and understanding that suicide can only be understood and reconciled in God's great love. In his letter inaugurating the Jubilee Year of Mercy 2016, he writes: '*It is indeed my wish that the Jubilee be a living experience of the closeness of the Father, whose tenderness is almost tangible…*' I believe that suicide victims would be first in line for this transforming tenderness of God's mercy.

If not in hell, where are they?

When faced with the suicide of a loved one, we may assume the very worst of the person and of God: 'they have committed an unforgivable sin and must suffer the harsh consequences', goes the logic. The assumption is that they have cut themselves off from God the unforgiving and condemning judge, so that there is no way back, escape or remedy. We have this black and white view: they are lost or found, in hell or in heaven. But in reality it is more like shades of grey. Maybe there is another place between heaven and hell specifically for the healing of suicide? This 'emergency care unit', an intense healing of hurt or wounds, is where Christ works intensely to love wounded people back to wholeness.

The good news is that God can't help being caring (God *is* mercy) and still works with them beyond death. God has walked with them all their lives and is still with them through death. Pope Benedict XVI preached that not even Judas is damned to hell: 'Even though he went to hang himself (cf. Mt. 27:5), it is not up to us to judge his gesture, substituting ourselves for the infinitely merciful and just God.'[21] In this sense there is nothing, not even suicide, or no place, not even hell, beyond the reach of God. There are no lengths to which God will not go to save a person from this alienation or isolation that we call hell. I find this consoling that my brother, who was a good person, should not be defined by suicide.

St John Vianney consoles a wife bereaved by suicide using words that I really like: 'Between the parapet of the bridge and the water he had time to make an act of contrition.' It highlights the fact that it is never too late and that God is always there to catch the suicidal person in this extreme act, even if they themselves don't pray or deserve it. God can change time to allow forgiveness to take place; there is no 'too late' or 'too far gone'. Thought of my own brother's despairing final moments is transformed knowing that God always reaches out to catch the fall, to make that impossible 11th hour intervention, and to save from total darkness. God the merciful seeks to understand and heal the person, regardless of their actions and destructive behaviour. God is moved by the their suffering and despair and suffers with them in this desperate hour.[22] God is love or in this case forgiving mercy that reaches out, just like the Prodigal Son's father (Luke 15:11-32). The mad extravagance of the Father's love heals the son's wounds and makes the way back possible. We all belong in our Father's house and every road eventually brings us back home. God never gives up, even if we do.

While ideas about hell, damnation and being lost forever abound, the Church and the Bible don't support the definitive loss of anyone. In fact the Creed affirms that Christ descended into Hell to release the souls there, that nothing was beyond the power of Christ's resurrection. A more helpful way to think of suicide would be as an extra journey where the suffering of these tormented souls is resolved through direct contact with Christ's healing love.

It is a place of transformation and freedom, *intensive care for the soul* if you like, where they are freed from their chains.[23]

Ritual, symbol and pilgrimage

The careful use of rituals, symbols and prayer can really help your bereavement process in later phases. It is all about timing. Initially present yourself to God with a prayer asking for the healing or grace you want, but being open to what God wants for you, i.e. 'Give me some peace of mind with this terrible grief, but not my will but yours be done'. Select a symbol of the person whom you have lost, something that evokes them strongly i.e. a piece of clothing, a photo, a personal item. Set yourself some physical challenge that will stretch you (not one that is impossible), but that has some ascetical quality and some meditative element. Carry your symbol with you on this challenge. For example, walk to a special place, climb a mountain, swim a certain number of lengths in a pool, cycle a route that is special for you. Prepare a ritual that has meaning for you, e.g. burning a piece of the person's clothing, burying a journal of your grief, refurbish a favourite chair of your beloved, prayerfully dispose of their personal effects or honour a special photo.

Afterwards, do a simple purification with water, e.g. having a long shower, a dip in a pool or in the sea. Remember your birth in the Spirit (e.g. baptism) and how you are a child of God, renewed by Christ. Finally, reflect on the whole process to see where you have been moved, if there is a new freedom in you or not, or simply where God has been present. Write up your reflections in a private journal. You may have to repeat this process a number of times, adjusting certain elements as you go. Notice where you might be getting stuck and pray for help with that part.

The funeral service, anniversary masses and other milestones are an important part of the healing; it is a good way to express grief and get support; it provides meaning for this senseless act. It can help to acknowledge publically that it was suicide, that the person was good, yet without idealising suicide. A Church funeral rite designed for suicide is very useful[24].

Living a positive aspect

One thing I found useful to commemorate the loved one was to take a positive aspect of their personality (for me it was my brother's sense of humour) and make it my own. That is, use it to make yourself a better person using a characteristic of the deceased. This has the advantage of being a very positive memorial of the person, celebrating their life, and being a positive element in your life for the future. It allows them to live on in you and to have a positive expression that adds to your personality and means they still have an influence on the world.

The deceased wants you to live

A lot of suicide survivors report that they often come to a point of wishing they had died or not wanting to live any longer without the person. Sometimes the darkness is so intense they think of taking their own life. A crucial element of moving on in a positive way is understanding that even though the person chose to die in taking their life, they do not wish you to die (this can be difficult as emotionally their dying feels like a death sentence for you). The person who dies by suicide is normally in such great pain that they can't think of anyone else and they kill themselves in order to get away from the pain, not from you[25].

It is very common to ask 'where are they?' and 'how are they present to me now?' In a very profound sense they are enclosed in the mercy of God, as Pope Francis says:

The Father, with patience, love, hope and mercy, had never for a second stopped thinking about [his wayward offspring], and as soon as he sees him still far off, he runs out to meet him and embraces him with tenderness, the tenderness of God, without a word of reproach. ... God is always waiting for us, He never grows tired.[26]

The deceased are released from their torment, and are lovingly watching over you and praying for you. They don't want you to live your life in misery and endless grief; they want you to move on in a way where they are remembered fondly but not painfully missed. They especially don't want you to be paying the price for their death, or living on the edge of suicide yourself. Pray to your lost loved one and seek their permission to go on living; to let go of them in a healthy way (not forgetting them), and to live your life in peace.

Grief is a journey
The Spanish word for 'journey' or 'way' is 'camino', and this image accurately reflects the bereavement process. I walked the Spanish pilgrimage route, the Camino, in 2011 as a tribute for my brother. I walked 500 miles, had 5 injuries and was out there for 5 weeks. On one level it was a terrible ordeal of blisters, pain and thirst, but on a deeper level it was enormously significant for my healing.

God had a plan for me and a big part of it was letting go of control, slowing down and really listening to myself. Instead of trying to avoid the pain, I learnt to walk with and through it.

Like a lot of grief my walk seemed largely meaningless. I felt like I was walking in the dark for most of the pilgrimage. That was until God kicked in right at the 11th hour. On a rocky cape near the town of Finisterre (which means 'End of the World') everything suddenly came together in a simple ritual. I found myself burning my brother's shirt, which I had carried the entire walk, in an unexpected cathartic moment. It hurt a lot but I was released from the burden of grief and I felt a new inner peace. My brother was present to me in a new, very intimate way, and I was happy for the first time in a long time.

Setting out on your grief journey you have to make an act of faith in yourself, in God and in being open to whatever happens. The fact that you are travelling, in movement, is key. The journey is done one step at a time. No matter if you are currently living in hell (Winston Churchill once said: 'if you are going through Hell, just keep going!'), this means that you are on the road out of it. You don't have to feel great; you just have to realise that surviving is enough. Getting through a day is a mountain climbed, carrying your burden you stagger initially but it becomes little by little more manageable, and being on the road is infinitely preferable to a slow death stuck at home. Each small step matters, you walk your unique journey and hope beckons. Keeping the flame of hope alive through the darkest nights is an art. Prayer is a primal cry for compassion, and God is a parent who waits anxiously for us round the next corner. One day the pain will lessen, the burden will lighten. By embracing this journey you will be different and transformed in the light of revelation that removes fear of death and where we can embrace our loved ones.

A new person forged in suffering

The most important thing for me personally however, was that shouldering this cross taught me what it is to be human. I now understand the word 'compassion', as meaning 'to suffer with another'; literally sharing the 'passion' of others. I think I understand the nature of suffering and the humility involved in not judging others too readily. A lot of this is down to the paradoxical gifts in suicide: we come to know ourselves and God in suffering. Having some experience of the suicide trauma and the questions it raises, teaches one about the true nature of humanity. It means appreciating our mortality and the fragility of life; how important it is to be compassionate, not to judge, and to understand vulnerability and pain in its many disguises.

In this context, faith or spirituality is not an escape but a desperate search for meaning in the most meaningless of experiences. Belief in an afterlife suddenly makes sense. Finally, there are all the many hard won lessons such as 'you can't take responsibility for another's life', 'God works through this most difficult of human situations', and 'it is only in the mystery of faith that there are any answers'. These are the insights about life and death, love and suffering, which are not readily found in any textbook. I wouldn't have asked for this experience for myself or my family, but I am grateful for the blessings that have come out of it.

There is hope that one day you will get beyond grief, not that you will forget the deceased, but that you will live in this new reality, the 'new normal' with peace and joy. This can seem an impossible dream but it is possible with hope and more than a little faith. The essence of faith is that good can come out of bad, hope is born in despair and the winter of desolation is always followed by a springtime of hope. An inescapable part of the crucible of suffering is that it makes us different; it changes our hearts, and brings out compassion. Because you have been tested in fire, you can be merciful to others, you become more authentic and open and your experience becomes a way of helping others. Your suffering becomes a healing gift for others.[27]

Hope in the Resurrection

The Gospel story of the road to Emmaus is a suicide bereavement story (Luke 24:13-35). The two disciples trudge out of Jerusalem totally depressed and in despair as their lives and dreams have been shattered by the death of a loved one. The one they hoped in had been killed and they saw it as the end – no one comes back from death, they thought. Ironically it is the same Jesus who has overcome death who comforts them and gives new hope.

The resurrection is a crucial lifeline for a survivor of suicide, Christ has beaten even death. The awfulness and trauma of suicide can be healed in God, in the spirit (for it is a spiritual wound). Unbelievably, this situation of irreversible loss can be saved and restored. It seems impossible to believe, too good to be true, and yet it is the ultimate test of our faith, to trust there is meaning in deep darkness. Death is not the end and the power of God is greater that the bleakness of suicide.

God *always* gives us another chance, is not mean and capricious, but is loving and merciful. God who wants to heal and forgive, to restore the seemingly impossible, understands the awfulness of the suicide act and the devastating pain for the survivors. Just like the Emmaus disciples above, we have to let Jesus reinterpret the bereavement story for us. We tend to read it as a story of negativity and loss, but Jesus reads it in terms of the power of God. Only when it seems like everything is lost, that there is no meaning, does God weigh in with great love and compassion. The reality is those who have died are already with God in love, their suffering is over, and they are waiting for us to catch on to this divine 'rescue' (redemption). Your loved one has gone to God, is beyond time and suffering, and is fully assimilated to Christ in spirit. There is real consolation in that reality that love can win out, that death is not the end and everything is reconciled in God.

Bodily resurrection

Part of the awful trauma of suicide is that the person concerned has inflicted a great violence on their body to cause their death. I was spared seeing this but many survivors tell of the horror of discovering the body of their loved one and how this image haunts them. A broken and lifeless body can never be mended or put back together again, just as our lives are broken and smashed apart. However, a key aspect of the resurrection is that it is a resurrection of the body too, as we know from the appearances of the risen Jesus and how he emphasised his bodily nature, asking for fish, asking people to touch him and engaging with disciples and believers. Only God has this awesome power to restore people in such a fashion, to heal them of their mortal wounds and for them to live with God in heaven.

I have this outrageous, beyond my wildest wishes, hope that I will see my brother again. Indeed I would not wish for anything else in the world but this. Because he will be restored, redeemed, to his best self, his scars and burdens will have been removed and he will be shining like the sun, the light that is Christ.

I will see him coming towards me, he will have that smile on his face, he will be pointing at me, indicating to come forward that we might look at each other. I will be in tears, but he will be grinning broadly and welcoming me in to his new home, where we will be together with God forever. And I will not want for anything else.

Ignatian Rules of Thumb for Surviving Suicide[28]

- Remember that you are not your feelings: even though you feel truly awful and can barely function, keep reminding yourself that this is grief talking and not your real self. One day, you will get through all this and get back to your 'same but new' self.

- Use mindfulness or meditation to separate yourself from your feelings. Though this is very hard, especially in the beginning, it helps to reduce the tyranny of feelings. Use a short mantra or phrase like 'One day all of this will pass' to keep focused.

- There are two forces working on us all the time, one is life giving and the other is deadening. You can recognise life, optimism and hope in that it lifts the spirit; the deadening one is dry and empty heaviness, despair and negativity, which kills the spirit.

- Learn how to recognise those situations that are genuinely life giving and those that are not. Sometimes this takes a lot of courage to face down depression and lethargy.

- Act against those forces inside yourself that are negative, seductive and that lead towards depression.

- In the evening, look back over your day as if you were watching a movie of it (see the people, places and emotions). Try to find gratitude for any gifts you have received – even the darkest days have some light in them – and realise that you can work at being more positive.

- Don't make a decision when you are down, especially one that undermines your support structures. Rather when you are going through a tough time, don't change anything important and wait it out for a better day.

- Don't let negative feeling dictate your decisions, rather ask yourself 'If I was in good form, how would I decide'?

- Sometimes when you are not able for the demands of the day, try to take small steps, accomplish small things that you can do and see how far you get.

- Take time to make good (not rushed) decisions that help your recovery; decisions about getting help and support can seem scary but can bring a lot of good. You may have to act against the resistance you find in yourself.

Helpful Books

Kay Redfield Jamison, *An Unquiet Mind: A Memoir of Moods and Madness.* (New York: Vintage, 1996).

William Styron, *Darkness Visible.* (New York: Knopf Doubleday, 1992).

Alison Wertheimer, *A Special Scar: The Experience of People Bereaved by Suicide.* (London: Routledge, 2001).

Living with Suicide, Console Booklet. www.console.ie http://consolecounselling.co.uk/index.php/product/living-with-suicide-booklet

DB Biebel & SL Foster, *Finding Your Way after the Suicide of someone you Love.* (Michigan: Zondervan, 2005).

Brian Grogan SJ, *Where To From Here – A Christian Vision of life After Death.* (Dublin: Veritas, 2011).

Eric Marcus, *Why Suicide: Questions and Answers about Suicide, Suicide Prevention, and Coping with the Suicide of Someone You Know (2nd ed.).* (San Francisco: HarperOne, 2010).

(Endnotes)

1 Thanks to Kate (survivor), Conor (therapist) and Karen (reviewer) for their invaluable feedback and advice in writing this.

2 These Kübler-Ross stages were developed around the terminally ill and not specifically for the bereaved.

3 'I am not my feelings; my feelings come and go and I need to keep myself apart from them, otherwise I will suffer.' Anthony DeMello, *Awareness*, (New York: Image Books, 1990).

4 1 Peter 1:7.

5 Joyce Rupp's book on *Praying Our Goodbyes* (Eagle, 1988) is very useful on this, particularly Chapter 2 and the section "False Theories of Suffering (p.28)".

6 See the classic by Harold S Kushner, *When Bad Things Happen to Good People*, (New York: Avon Books, 1981).

7 It is consoling to realise that Jesus himself asks for a way out, showing his humanity. Lk 22:42.

8 Matthew 27:46. This cry is a fulfillment of Psalm 22:1.

9 Carmel McCarthy, *The Psalms – Human Voices of Prayer and Suffering*, (Dublin: Messenger Publications, 2012).

10 Take a bible story such as the rich young man, 'And Jesus, looking at him, loved him.' Mark 10:21, and put yourself in the story whereby Jesus looks at you. How would he look at you, what would he say?

11 Paraphrased from Anthony DeMello, *Sadhana. A Way to God*, (Colorado: Image Books, 1984) pp. 15-28.

12 This is crucial, not to be easily put off. People often don't understand suicide bereavement and you will have some doors closed to you, but you have to find others to open. Ironically, though the experience of being ejected from the AWARE group was traumatic, it was a huge advantage to discover Console. I had to use all of my mindfulness and CBT skills (not personalising it).

13 Support groups are provided by Console (www.console.ie) in the Republic of Ireland and Lighthouse (www.lighthousecharity.com) in the North.

14 Ignatius of Loyola would call this 'desolation', the signs of emptiness, obsession and darkness that indicate that you are moving away from God. The signs of 'Consolation' are the opposite: light, freedom and hope.

15 The fact that suicide victims are now buried in consecrated ground speaks volumes; the new Catechism of the Catholic Church has a much more pastoral and compassionate attitude; and Purgatory is no longer seen as exterior penal punishment but as 'becoming one with God' R McBrien, Catholicism. p.1168.

16 The New Catechism of the Catholic Church (CCC), 1992, Libreria Editrice Vaticana No's 2282 & 2283. However, note here the use of the word 'commit' suicide, implying a criminal act, and which is an unhelpful way to describe suicide. The language around suicide is very important and how it is described has larger implications.

17 'Psychiatric disorders, usually depression, or an intoxicant problem is pres-

ent in 90 % of people who take their own lives.' *Suicide In Ireland: A Global Perspective and A National Strategy*. www.aware.ie/online%20books/suicide.html.

18 CCC 1857, "Mortal sin is sin whose object is grave matter and which is also committed with full knowledge and deliberate consent.".

19 Irish Catholic Bishops' Conference pastoral letter 'Life is for Living – A Reflection on Suicide' 2004.

20 An important distinction is that in showing compassion for suicide victims and their families is not condoning the act of suicide itself or promoting it in any way. One only has to look at the devastation and immeasurable heartache left behind to realise the unquestionable negative consequences.

21 http://www.thedivinemercy.org/news/Christs-Betrayal-and-Divine-Mercy-2455

22 Walter Kasper, *Mercy: The Essence Of The Gospel And The Key To Christian Life* translated by William Madges, (New Jersey: Paulist Press, 2013).

23 For more see chapter 'Purgatory: Remedial Loving', Brian Grogan SJ, *Where To From Here*, (Dublin: Veritas, 2011) pp.128–134.

24 Flourish Worship Resource, http://www.wewillflourish.com/wp-content/uploads/2015/09/flourish-book.pdf

25 'Suicide is their attempt to escape pain and suffering', https://www.psychologytoday.com/blog/teen-angst/201210/understanding-suicide-and-self-harm.

26 Pope Francis, Homily on Divine Mercy Sunday, April 7, 2013.

27 DB Biebel & SL Foster *Finding Your Way after the Suicide of someone you Love*.

28 These Ignatian rules are taken from the spiritual Classic *The Spiritual Exercises of St Ignatius*, which have some very concrete wisdom about making decisions and coping with adversity.

The Sacred Heart Messenger

BEING THERE

A COMPANION ON THE PATHWAY OF ILLNESS

M

MARGARET T NAUGHTON

Author of *Walk With Me Into The Light: Some Comfort on the Journey Through Grief*

IGNATIAN BOOKSHOP

€3.99
WWW.MESSENGER.IE
TEL: 01-7758522

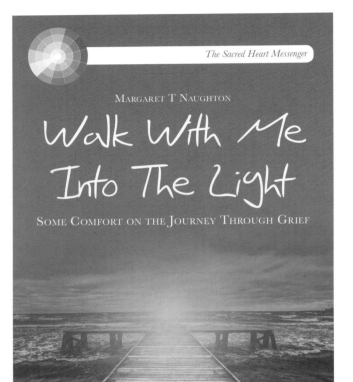

The Sacred Heart Messenger

Margaret T Naughton

Walk With Me Into The Light

Some Comfort on the Journey Through Grief

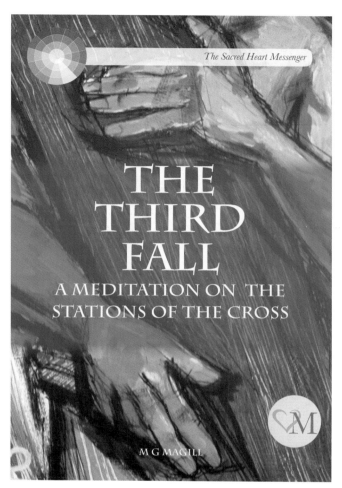

The Sacred Heart Messenger

THE THIRD FALL

A MEDITATION ON THE STATIONS OF THE CROSS

M G MAGILL

€3.99
WWW.MESSENGER.IE
TEL: 01-7758522

WWW.MESSENGER.IE
TEL: 01-7758522